Exploring T

Psychology's Most Intresting

Introduction .... Page 3

Chapter 1 - Milgram's obedience studies .... Page 5

Chapter 2 – The Stanford prison experiment .... Page 10

Chapter 3 – The Bobo doll experiment .... Page 14

Chapter 4 – The Little Albert experiment .... Page 18

Chapter 5 – The Marshmallow test .... Page 21

Chapter 6 - The Hawthorne effect .... Page 24

Chapter 7 – Asch's Conformity experiments .... Page 27

Chapter 8 – The Stroop effect .... Page 31

Chapter 9 – The Bystander Effect .... Page 34

Chapter 10 – Harlows monkey experiment .... Page 37

Chapter 11 – The Good Samaritan .... Page 41

Chapter 12 – False Consensus Study .... Page 44

Chapter 13 – The case of Henry Molaison .... Page 47

@TheLittleBookOfPsychology

Introduction

Psychology is the scientific study of the mind and behaviour. It seeks to understand and explain various aspects of human thought, emotion, perception, motivation, learning, and social interaction. Psychologists employ a variety of research methods, including experiments, surveys, observations, and case studies, to explore and analyse how individuals and group's function.

Psychology not only contributes to our understanding of individual and collective behaviour but also has practical applications in areas such as therapy, counselling, education, business, and healthcare. It plays a crucial role in helping individuals lead more fulfilling lives, improving mental health, and contributing to our overall knowledge of what it means to be human.

Psychologists establish cause-and-effect relationships by manipulating independent variables, randomly assigning participants to control and experimental groups, and measuring changes in the dependent variables. The controlled conditions, including the use of a control group, help isolate the impact of the manipulated variable. Rigorous measurement, replication, and statistical analysis contribute to the reliability and validity of experimental findings. Through manipulation and observation, experiments provide a robust method for researchers to draw causal inferences about the relationships between variables in psychology and other scientific disciplines.

This book delves into some of the most captivating psychology experiments ever conducted, offering insightful analyses of their methodologies and outcomes. From Milgram's obedience studies to the Stanford prison experiment and beyond, each study is explored in detail, providing readers with a comprehensive understanding of the research design and its implications. The book goes further to critically evaluate the significance and impact of these experiments, fostering a nuanced appreciation for the complexities of human behaviour uncovered through rigorous psychological inquiry.

Chapter 1 – Milgram's obedience studies (1961)

Stanley Milgram's experiments aimed to investigate how far people were willing to obey authority figures, even when doing so conflicted with their personal morals and values. Milgram was inspired to conduct these experiments in response to the atrocities committed by the Nazis during World War II, and he wanted to understand how ordinary people could be persuaded to engage in such heinous acts.

The participants in the study were led to believe that they were taking part in a study examining the effects of punishment on learning. The true aim of Milgram's study was to examine participants' obedience to authority and how far they were willing to go in administering increasingly intense electric shocks, despite the apparent distress and protests from the learner. The study also aimed to understand the factors that influenced people's obedience to authority figures, even when it involved potentially harming others.

Milgram's experiments involved a "teacher" (the participant) and a "learner" (a confederate of the experimenter). The teacher was instructed to administer electric shocks to the learner every time the learner made a mistake on a memory task. The shocks started at a low level and increased in intensity with each mistake. Unbeknownst to the teacher, the learner was not actually receiving any shocks, but was instead pretending to be in pain.

This deception was necessary in order to create a sense of tension and pressure in the participants, which would simulate the real-world situations in which people might be asked to obey authority figures.

Milgram also used various manipulations to test the limits of obedience, such as changing the proximity of the teacher and learner, or having the experimenter give different types of commands. Milgram measured the obedience of participants by recording how far they were willing to go in administering the shocks.

The results of Milgram's experiments were shocking, with many participants administering shocks all the way up to the maximum voltage level, even when the learner appeared to be in extreme pain. Milgram concluded that people are more likely to obey authority figures than to question their instructions, even if doing so conflicts with their own moral compass.

This implies that humans have a deeply ingrained need to conform and obey social norms and rules, even when those norms and rules may be harmful or immoral.

Milgram's experiments also suggest that humans may be more easily swayed by authority figures than by their own critical thinking and ethical judgment. This can have significant implications for how we understand human behaviour in a variety of contexts, such as politics, religion, and social conformity.

Furthermore, Milgram's experiments suggest that human behaviour is not solely determined by individual personality traits or characteristics but is also heavily influenced by situational factors such as the presence of authority figures and the expectations of social roles. This highlights the complex interplay between individual psychology and social context in shaping human behaviour.

Milgram's experiments were ground-breaking and innovative at the time they were conducted. Milgram's research shed light on an important and previously unexplored aspect of human behaviour. The experiments had a significant impact on the field of psychology and have influenced subsequent research on obedience and conformity.

A strength of Milgram's experiments is that they were highly controlled. Milgram was able to manipulate and observe the variables he was interested in, which increases the internal validity of the study by reducing the influence of extraneous variables.

However, one weakness of Milgram's experiments is that they lacked ecological validity. They were conducted in a laboratory setting and involved a highly artificial task. This raises questions about whether the results of the study can be generalised to real-world situations.

Another weakness of Milgram's experiments is that the sample was not representative of the general population. The participants were predominantly white, male, and middle-class, which limits the generalisability of the study and raises questions about whether the results can be applied to other groups.

Additionally, although Milgram took steps to ensure that participants were not subjected to long-term harm, the psychological distress that some participants experienced during the study raises ethical concerns about the use of deception and the potential harm caused to participants.

Finally, the highly controlled nature of the study and the use of deception may have led some participants to guess the true nature of the study and alter their behaviour accordingly. This raises concerns about the validity of the study and whether the results are a true reflection of participants' obedience levels in real-world situations.

Overall, Milgram's experiments have had a significant impact on the field of psychology and have led to important discussions about the nature of obedience and conformity. Although, the study also has several weaknesses, which limit the generalisability and validity of the results.

Chapter 2 – The Stanford prison experiment by Zimbardo (1971)

The aim of the Stanford prison experiment was to investigate how readily people would conform to the roles of guard and prisoner in a simulated prison environment. Specifically, the experiment sought to examine the psychological effects of power dynamics and authority on the behaviour of individuals within a social group.

To carry out the experiment, researcher Philip Zimbardo and his team recruited 24 male college students to participate in a two-week simulation of a prison environment. The participants were randomly assigned to the roles of guard or prisoner and were placed in a mock prison located in the basement of Stanford University's psychology building.

The experiment was designed to be highly realistic, with guards given uniforms and sunglasses to conceal their identity, and prisoners subjected to arrest, booking, and incarceration procedures. Zimbardo and his team observed the behaviour of the participants and recorded their interactions using video cameras and audio equipment.

The results of the Stanford prison experiment revealed that both the guards and prisoners quickly became immersed in their roles and began exhibiting extreme and sometimes abusive behaviours.

The guards became increasingly authoritarian and began using their power to control and manipulate the prisoners. They subjected the prisoners to psychological abuse, including harassment, degradation, and humiliation.

The prisoners, on the other hand, became passive and compliant, with some developing symptoms of depression and anxiety. Some even began to identify with their roles as prisoners, despite the artificial nature of the situation.

The experiment was terminated after only six days, as the behaviour of the participants had become too extreme and concerning. The results of the experiment shed light on the power of social roles and the potential for individuals to be influenced by authority figures and group dynamics.

The Stanford prison experiment suggests that humans have a strong tendency to conform to social roles and to be influenced by authority figures. The study demonstrates the profound impact that power dynamics and situational factors can have on individuals, even when they are placed in an artificial environment.

The experiment also highlights the potential for abusive and harmful behaviours to arise within groups when there is a power differential and a lack of oversight or accountability. This suggests that humans have the capacity for both prosocial and antisocial behaviour, and that situational factors play a significant role in determining which behaviours are expressed.

Overall, the Stanford prison experiment provides insights into the complex interplay between individual psychology and social dynamics and raises important questions about the ethics of research involving human subjects.

The study was highly controlled and simulated a realistic prison environment, which helped increase the internal validity of the results. Additionally, the study produced rich qualitative data, including video and audio recordings of participant behaviour and interactions.

Despite its significant impact, the Stanford prison experiment has been the subject of significant criticism due to its lack of proper ethical controls. The experiment has been described as unethical because many participants experienced psychological distress during the study. Furthermore, the sample size of the study was small and consisted only of male college students, which limits the generalisability of the results.

Another weakness of the experiment is the lack of proper oversight and accountability. The researchers themselves took on the roles of prison administrators, which may have led to experimenter bias. There are also concerns about the validity of the results, with some arguing that the artificial nature of the situation means that the behaviours observed in the study may not accurately reflect real-world behaviours. Finally, some have suggested that the results of the study may have been influenced by demand characteristics, as participants may have altered their behaviour in response to their understanding of the experiment's purpose.

Chapter 3 – The Bobo doll experiment by Bandura (1961)

The Bobo doll experiments were a series of studies conducted by psychologist Albert Bandura in the 1960s. The aim of the study was to investigate the role of observation and imitation in the acquisition of aggressive behavior in children.

In the experiments, children were shown a video of an adult model engaging in aggressive behavior towards a Bobo doll, a large inflatable doll with a weighted base that would spring back up when knocked over. The adult model would hit, kick, and verbally berate the doll. Following this, the children were allowed to play with the doll themselves while being observed by researchers.

Bandura varied the conditions of the study in several ways, including changing the gender of the model, the type of aggression displayed, and the level of punishment administered to the model. The children's behavior with the doll was then observed and recorded.

In the Bobo doll experiments, Bandura found that children who had observed the aggressive model were significantly more likely to engage in similar aggressive behaviors themselves when given the opportunity to play with the doll. The children who had not seen the aggressive model, on the other hand, were less likely to engage in aggressive behavior towards the doll.

Bandura also found that the level of aggression displayed by the model, as well as the consequences of the model's behavior, had an impact on the children's behavior. Children who had seen the model receive punishment for their aggressive behavior were less likely to imitate the model's actions.

These results supported Bandura's social learning theory, which proposes that individuals learn new behaviors by observing others and imitating their actions. The study also highlighted the importance of environmental factors, such as media exposure, in the development of aggressive behavior in children.

The Bobo doll experiment suggested that human behavior is heavily influenced by observation and imitation of others. It implies that individuals can learn new behaviors, including aggressive behaviors, simply by observing others engage in them. This highlights the role of the environment, including the media and social interactions, in shaping human behavior.

Moreover, the study demonstrated that the consequences of behavior can also influence human actions. In other words, if people witness negative consequences for certain behaviors, they may be less likely to engage in those behaviors themselves. This implies that human behavior is not solely determined by innate tendencies or traits, but also by environmental and situational factors.

Overall, the Bobo doll experiment indicates that human nature is not fixed, but is rather shaped by various social and environmental factors. It suggests that humans have the ability to learn and adapt their behavior based on the social context and consequences of their actions.

One of the main strengths of the study is its high level of control and rigor. The use of a standardized video of the adult model's behavior ensured that all participants were exposed to the same aggressive stimuli, increasing the internal validity of the study. Moreover, the study produced a wealth of quantitative data, including measures of the number and type of aggressive behaviors exhibited by children.

However, the study has also faced criticisms. One of the main weaknesses is its limited generalizability, as the study only included a relatively small sample of children from a specific geographic location and cultural background. The study also lacked ecological validity, as the setting of the experiment was artificial and may not reflect real-life situations. Furthermore, some have argued that the aggressive behavior exhibited by the children in the study was influenced by demand characteristics or experimenter bias, as the children may have behaved in a way that they believed was expected of them. Finally, the study has been criticized for its ethics, as some have questioned the ethics of exposing children to aggressive stimuli and the potential harm that this may have caused.

Chapter 4 – The Little Albert experiment by Watson & Rayner (1919)

The aim of the Little Albert experiment, conducted by John Watson and Rosalie Rayner in 1920, was to investigate whether a child could be conditioned to develop a phobia of a previously neutral object through classical conditioning. More specifically, the researchers wanted to test the hypothesis that emotions, such as fear, could be learned through the pairing of a neutral stimulus, in this case a white rat, with an unconditioned stimulus, such as a loud noise. The experiment was conducted on a nine-month-old infant named Albert, who had no prior fear of rats or similar objects.

The method of the experiment involved exposing Albert to various stimuli, including a white rat, a rabbit, a dog, a monkey, and masks, while recording his emotional responses. Initially, Albert showed no fear of the rat or the other objects. The researchers then paired the presentation of the rat with the loud noise, which caused Albert to become startled and cry. This pairing was repeated several times, and eventually Albert began to show fear not only of the rat, but also of other similar objects.

The pairing of the rat with a loud noise resulted in Albert developing a conditioned fear response not only to the rat but also to similar objects. The fear response was characterized by crying, attempting to crawl away, and clinging to his mother when exposed to the previously neutral stimulus, indicating that emotional responses could be learned through classical conditioning. This was a significant finding in the field of psychology, as it demonstrated the potential of classical conditioning to shape emotional responses and behavior.

The study suggests that humans may have an innate capacity for learning emotional responses through conditioning, which could have implications for the development of phobias and other emotional disorders. The study also highlights the importance of early experiences in shaping emotional responses, as Albert's fear of the rat and similar objects developed during his infancy.

The Little Albert experiment has been criticized for its ethical considerations. The use of an infant as a subject and the deliberate induction of fear in the child raises serious ethical concerns, and it is very unlikely that such a study would be approved by an Institutional Review Board today. Another weakness of the study is that the experiment was not well-controlled, and some aspects of the experimental design may have influenced the results. For example, the researchers conducting the experiment were also the ones who were conditioning Albert, which may have led to experimenter bias. Additionally, the study only involved one subject, which limits the generalizability of the findings.

On the other hand, one strength of the Little Albert experiment is that it contributed to the development of the theory of classical conditioning, which has been widely used in psychological research and practice. The study demonstrated that emotional responses could be learned through classical conditioning, which has been an important finding in the field of psychology. Furthermore, the study has been influential in raising ethical concerns about the use of human subjects in research, leading to the development of ethical guidelines for conducting research with human subjects.

Overall, while the Little Albert experiment has significant ethical concerns and methodological limitations, it has also contributed to our understanding of the role of conditioning in emotional responses and has had a lasting impact on the field of psychology.

Chapter 5 – The Marshmallow test by Mischel (1972)

The Marshmallow Test, also known as the Stanford Marshmallow Experiment, aimed to investigate the ability of children to delay gratification. The study was conducted in 1972 by psychologist Walter Mischel and his colleagues at Stanford University.

The method involved presenting children with a choice between a small, immediate reward (such as one marshmallow) or a larger reward (such as two marshmallows) if they were willing to wait for a certain period of time. The children were left alone in a room with the marshmallow and were told that if they waited until the experimenter returned, they could receive the larger reward. The researchers then observed the children's behavior and recorded how long they were able to delay gratification. The study aimed to investigate whether children who were able to delay gratification had better outcomes later in life, such as better academic achievement and social skills.

The results of the Marshmallow Test showed that the ability to delay gratification was associated with better outcomes in various areas of life. The children who were able to resist the temptation of the immediate reward and wait for the larger reward were found to have better academic performance, higher SAT scores, better social skills, and less incidence of obesity. Additionally, the study found that the ability to delay gratification was linked to self-control, which is an important aspect of emotional intelligence.

The findings of the Marshmallow Test have been replicated in subsequent studies, providing support for the idea that the ability to delay gratification is an important predictor of success in life.

One strength of the Marshmallow Test is that it was a longitudinal study that followed the participants over a long period of time, allowing the researchers to observe the long-term effects of the ability to delay gratification. Additionally, the study had a large sample size, which enhances the generalizability of the findings. Furthermore, the experimenters used a standardized procedure to administer the test to the participants, which increases the reliability of the results.

However, the Marshmallow Test has been criticized for various weaknesses. One limitation is that the sample was drawn from a specific population, which was predominantly white, middle-class, and living in suburban areas. This limits the generalizability of the findings to other populations with different backgrounds and socio-economic statuses. Another criticism is that the test only measured the ability to delay gratification in a single context, and therefore may not accurately reflect an individual's ability to delay gratification in other contexts. Finally, the study did not take into account other factors, such as personality traits, that may have influenced the ability to delay gratification and the outcomes observed in the participants.

Chapter 6 - The Hawthorne effect

It's important to note that the Hawthorne effect is not a specific experiment, but rather a phenomenon that was observed in several experiments conducted at the Hawthorne Works factory in the 1920s and 1930s.

The primary aim of these experiments was to study the effects of various environmental factors on worker productivity, such as changes in lighting, temperature, and work hours. The researchers were interested in determining whether altering these factors would result in improvements in worker productivity.

The method used in these experiments involved manipulating the environmental conditions of the workplace and observing the resulting changes in worker productivity. For example, in one experiment, the lighting levels were increased, and in another, they were decreased. The researchers then recorded the changes in worker productivity that occurred as a result of these alterations in the environmental conditions. In some of the experiments, the researchers also observed how changes in work hours or breaks affected productivity.

Although the specific experiments varied in their design and focus, they all shared the goal of investigating the relationship between environmental factors and worker productivity.

The researchers observed changes in worker productivity that were difficult to explain based solely on the environmental factors that were manipulated. For example, in one experiment, worker productivity increased when the lighting levels were increased, but it also increased when the lighting levels were decreased. This led the researchers to suspect that other factors, such as social and psychological factors, were influencing the workers' behavior and performance.

The Hawthorne effect refers specifically to the changes in behavior and performance that were observed as a result of being studied, rather than any specific findings or results. The effect has since been observed in a wide range of social science research studies and is now widely recognized as an important consideration in study design and interpretation.

The effect highlights the importance of considering the role of the researcher and research process itself when interpreting study results. Researchers must be aware of the potential for their presence and influence to affect study participants, which can lead to changes in behavior and performance that are not solely related to the experimental manipulations.

Overall, the Hawthorne effect demonstrates the complexity of human behavior and the need to consider a wide range of factors when studying and interpreting human actions and responses.

Chapter 7 – Asch's Conformity experiments (1951)

Asch's conformity experiment aimed to investigate the extent to which people conform to the opinions and behaviors of a group. Specifically, the study sought to determine if and how social pressure from a majority group could influence the judgments and decisions of an individual.

The study involved a group of participants who were brought into a room with several confederates (people who were secretly working with the researcher). The participants were told that they were participating in a study on visual perception and were asked to look at a series of lines of varying lengths and indicate which line was the same length as a reference line. However, only one participant was actually being tested, while the others were confederates.

In each trial, the group was asked to give their answers one by one. The confederates were instructed to give incorrect answers on a certain number of trials to see if the participant would conform and also give an incorrect answer. The study varied the number of confederates in the group, as well as the unanimity of their answers.

The study measured the degree to which the participant conformed to the group's incorrect answers, as well as the factors that influenced their decisions to conform or deviate from the group. The experiment was designed to test the extent to which individuals would change their opinions and behaviors to fit in with a group, even when they knew the group was wrong.

The results of the Asch conformity experiment showed that a significant proportion of participants (about 75%) conformed to the incorrect answers given by the confederates at least once during the experiment. However, not all participants conformed on every trial, and some participants never conformed at all.

The level of conformity was influenced by various factors, including the size of the majority group, the unanimity of their answers, and the difficulty of the task. Participants were more likely to conform when the majority group was larger, more unanimous, and when the task was more ambiguous or difficult.

Furthermore, follow-up experiments found that conformity was reduced when participants had an ally in the group who gave the correct answer, or when participants were allowed to write down their answers instead of giving them verbally.

The results of the Asch conformity experiment imply that human nature is susceptible to social influence and the pressures of conformity. The study demonstrated that people are willing to compromise their own beliefs and conform to group norms, even when they know that the group is wrong. This suggests that social influence can have a powerful effect on human behavior, and that individuals may prioritize social acceptance and belonging over their own independent judgment.

However, the study also revealed that not all individuals conform equally, and that the level of conformity is influenced by various factors. This implies that human nature is complex and multifaceted, and that individual differences and situational factors also play a role in shaping human behavior.

One of the strengths of the study is that it was conducted in a controlled laboratory setting, allowing for careful manipulation of variables and systematic measurement of outcomes. This experimental design increases the internal validity of the study, meaning that the results are more likely to accurately reflect the impact of social influence on conformity. Additionally, the study used a large sample size, increasing the statistical power of the findings and making it more representative of the general population.

However, one weakness of the Asch conformity experiment is that it has limited external validity. The study was conducted in a laboratory setting, which is an artificial environment that may not accurately reflect real-world situations. Furthermore, the participants in the study were all male college students, which raises questions about the generalizability of the findings to other populations. Additionally, some critics have argued that the study lacks ecological validity, as the task involved making judgments about visual stimuli rather than more meaningful or relevant decisions.

Another weakness of the study is that it has ethical concerns. The participants were deceived about the true nature of the study, and they may have experienced stress or discomfort as a result of the manipulation. This raises important ethical questions about the use of deception in research and the potential harm that may result from such practices.

Overall, while the Asch conformity experiment provides valuable insights into the dynamics of social influence and conformity, it is important to consider the limitations and ethical concerns associated with the study.

Chapter 8 – The Stroop effect by Ridley (1935)

The Stroop effect is a classic cognitive psychology experiment named after John Ridley Stroop. The aim of the Stroop effect is to investigate the effect of interference on a person's reaction time in performing a task.

The method used in the experiment involves presenting participants with a list of color words, such as "red," "blue," and "green," written in an ink color that either matches or conflicts with the word's meaning. Participants are then instructed to name the color of the ink, while ignoring the meaning of the word. The time taken to complete the task is measured and compared between the two conditions (matching and conflicting ink colors). The difference in reaction time between the two conditions is considered the Stroop effect. The Stroop effect is believed to occur because reading is an automatic process that interferes with the task of naming the ink color.

The results of the Stroop effect experiment showed that participants took longer to name the ink color when the word's meaning conflicted with the ink color (e.g., the word "red" written in blue ink) compared to when the word's meaning matched the ink color (e.g., the word "red" written in red ink). This suggests that reading is an automatic process that interferes with the task of naming the ink color. Participants were slower and less accurate in the conflicting condition, indicating that their attention was captured by the word's meaning and not solely focused on the ink color. The Stroop effect has been replicated in numerous studies and is considered a robust phenomenon in cognitive psychology.

The Stroop effect implies that humans have a limited capacity for attention and that cognitive processes can interfere with each other. Specifically, the Stroop effect demonstrates how automatic and involuntary reading processes can interfere with the more effortful and voluntary task of identifying colors. This highlights the complexity of human cognition and the role of attention in performing cognitive tasks. Additionally, the Stroop effect has been used to study attentional processes in various clinical populations, such as individuals with attention deficit hyperactivity disorder (ADHD) or traumatic brain injury. Overall, the Stroop effect suggests that understanding how attentional processes work can help us better understand how the human brain processes information.

The Stroop effect is a well-known and frequently replicated phenomenon, which adds to its strength as a reliable and robust experimental paradigm. The original study by John Ridley Stroop in 1935 used a relatively large sample size and a well-controlled experimental design, which also enhances the credibility of the findings. The Stroop effect has also been widely used to investigate various aspects of cognition, such as attention, inhibition, and interference. This has led to numerous applications in clinical and research settings, including the assessment of cognitive deficits in various patient populations.

However, there are also some limitations to the Stroop effect as a measure of cognitive processing. One criticism is that it may not be a pure measure of attentional interference since the task may involve additional cognitive processes, such as response selection and working memory. Another limitation is that the Stroop effect may be influenced by individual differences, such as reading ability and language proficiency. Furthermore, some studies have found that the size of the Stroop effect can be influenced by various factors, such as task difficulty, stimulus duration, and experimental context. Overall, while the Stroop effect is a valuable tool for studying cognitive processes, it is important to consider its limitations and interpret the results with caution.

Chapter 9 – The Bystander Effect (1964)

In 1964, a women named Kitty Genovese was murdered outside her apartment building in New York City, and it was reported that 38 witnesses saw or heard the attack but failed to intervene or call for help. This event brought the issue of bystander inaction to public attention and prompted social psychologists to investigate the phenomenon in more detail. The murder of Kitty Genovese became a symbol of the bystander effect and highlighted the importance of understanding the psychological factors that influence people's behavior in emergency situations.

The aim of the bystander effect experiments was to investigate the influence of the presence of other people on an individual's likelihood of intervening in an emergency situation. The method involved placing participants in staged emergency situations, such as hearing a person in distress or witnessing a staged seizure, and observing their response when alone or in the presence of other people. The study sought to determine if the presence of others decreased the likelihood of intervention, as well as to identify the factors that might influence an individual's decision to intervene.

In one experiment, participants were placed in a room and asked to fill out a questionnaire. Unbeknownst to the participants, smoke was then pumped into the room through a vent, creating a visible and obvious source of potential danger.

The researchers varied the number of participants in the room from one to three and measured how long it took for them to report the smoke. They found that participants who were alone reported the smoke much more quickly than those who were in a group. In fact, when there were other people in the room, some participants didn't report the smoke at all, assuming that someone else would take responsibility for reporting the danger.

The researchers concluded that the larger the group, the less likely any individual was to intervene and offer help. This phenomenon is known as "diffusion of responsibility," where individuals feel less personal responsibility to help when others are present. Additionally, the researchers found that the presence of a confederate who intentionally did not help greatly decreased the likelihood that other bystanders would intervene. This suggests that social cues and modeling behavior can have a significant impact on whether or not people offer help in emergency situations.

The bystander effect experiments have several strengths. First, the study had a high degree of control over the experimental conditions, which increased the internal validity of the findings. Second, the study used a large sample of participants, making it more representative of the general population. Third, the study utilized both laboratory and field experiments, which increased the generalizability of the findings.

However, there were also several weaknesses of the study. First, the experimental conditions used in the laboratory experiments were somewhat artificial and may not accurately reflect real-world situations. Second, the study did not take into account individual differences in personality or other factors that could affect the likelihood of helping behavior. Third, the study primarily focused on the role of the number of bystanders, and did not address other factors that could affect the likelihood of helping behavior, such as the relationship between the victim and the bystander.

Chapter 10 – Harlows monkey experiment (1950)

The aim of Harlow's monkey experiments was to investigate the effects of maternal separation and social isolation on infant monkeys. Harlow wanted to test the prevailing belief at the time that food was the primary source of attachment between mother and child.

His method involved separating infant monkeys from their mothers shortly after birth and placing them in cages with two surrogate mothers - one made of wire and one made of cloth. The wire mother provided food for the infant, while the cloth mother did not. The study was conducted in several phases, with Harlow observing how the infants responded to the two surrogate mothers and how they interacted with other monkeys when reintroduced to a social environment.

In Harlow's monkey experiments, the results showed that the monkeys spent most of their time clinging to the cloth mother instead of the wire mother, even when the wire mother provided nourishment. The monkeys would only go to the wire mother to feed and then immediately return to the cloth mother. The experiment also revealed that the monkeys reared by the cloth mother were less anxious and better adjusted than those reared by the wire mother. These results challenged the prevailing belief at the time that attachment was purely based on nourishment and instead showed the importance of contact comfort and physical touch in the development of attachment.

The results of the Harlow's monkey experiments suggest that attachment is not simply a matter of providing for an infant's physical needs, such as food, but also involves the provision of comfort and security through social interaction. The monkeys in the study showed a preference for the cloth mother surrogate, even when it did not provide food, over the wire mother surrogate that did provide food. This implies that attachment involves more than just the satisfaction of basic physiological needs, but also involves the provision of emotional support and social interaction.

The study also suggested that the formation of attachment bonds is influenced by early experiences. The monkeys who were raised without a mother figure, or with a harsh and unresponsive mother figure, showed abnormal behaviors and social deficits later in life, which were difficult to reverse even with later socialization experiences. This suggests that early experiences play a critical role in shaping later social development and attachment patterns.

Overall, the study highlights the importance of social interaction and emotional support in attachment formation, as well as the long-term effects of early experiences on social development.

Harlow's monkey experiments have been praised for their innovative and influential contribution to the field of psychology. One of the strengths of the study is that it challenged the traditional behaviorist view that the primary motivator of behavior is reinforcement. The study provided evidence that attachment and affection are powerful motivators, which is important in understanding human behavior. Another strength is that it demonstrated the importance of early maternal care in development. The findings have implications for child-rearing practices, as they suggest that physical contact and emotional warmth are essential for healthy development.

However, the study has also faced criticism for its ethical concerns. Harlow's use of severe deprivation and isolation has been condemned as cruel and inhumane, raising important ethical issues about animal welfare and the use of animals in research. Another limitation of the study is that it was conducted on monkeys and may not be generalizable to humans. Additionally, the small sample size and lack of a control group may have affected the validity of the study's findings.

Overall, while the study provided valuable insights into the importance of attachment and early maternal care, its ethical concerns and methodological limitations cannot be overlooked.

Chapter 11 – The Good Samaritan by Darley & Batson (1973)

The Good Samaritan Experiment was conducted by John Darley and Daniel Batson in 1973 to investigate the factors that influence helping behavior in people. The aim of the study was to test whether the context of a situation, the time pressure, and the personal characteristics of a person would impact their willingness to help someone in need. The method involved participants who were seminary students and were asked to deliver a speech about a religious topic in another building. Some were told they were running late and needed to hurry, while others were told they had plenty of time. On the way to the other building, participants passed a man slumped in a doorway, appearing to need help. The researchers observed whether the participants stopped to help the man, and whether the time pressure and personal characteristics affected their decision to help.

The results of the Good Samaritan Experiment showed that the likelihood of someone offering help to a person in distress depended on several factors. Participants who were told they were in a hurry were less likely to stop and help the person in need, regardless of whether they were seminary students or not. The number of people who passed by also had an impact, with those in a less crowded situation being more likely to stop and help. Finally, the topic of the sermon the participants had just heard (the parable of the Good Samaritan or a different topic) did not have a significant effect on whether they helped or not. Overall, the study suggests that situational factors can play a significant role in determining whether someone will offer help to another person in need.

The results of the Good Samaritan Experiment suggest that human nature is complex and context dependent. Despite the fact that all of the participants were seminary students training to be religious leaders, their behavior was not solely determined by their personal values or moral convictions. Instead, their behavior was influenced by situational factors such as the time pressure they were under. This suggests that people are not always able to act according to their beliefs or intentions, and that they can be swayed by external circumstances. It also implies that our behavior is not necessarily consistent across different situations, and that we may act differently depending on the context we find ourselves in. Overall, the study highlights the importance of understanding the context in which behavior occurs, and the ways in which situational factors can shape our actions.

The Good Samaritan experiment had several strengths, including the use of a realistic scenario that mirrored real-life situations where people may need help. Additionally, the study had a high degree of experimental control, as the researchers were able to manipulate the time pressure variable and observe its effect on helping behavior. However, there were also some weaknesses to the study. The study was conducted in an artificial laboratory setting, which may not fully capture the complexities and nuances of real-life helping situations. Additionally, the study may have lacked ecological validity, as the participants may have known that they were being observed and may have behaved differently as a result. Finally, the study only looked at helping behavior in a specific group of individuals, in one specific context and may not be generalizable to other groups or situations where helping behavior may be necessary.

Chapter 12 – False Consensus Study By Ross (1977)

The aim of Ross' False Consensus Effect study was to investigate the tendency of people to overestimate the extent to which others share their beliefs, attitudes, and behaviors, also known as the false consensus effect. The method involved asking participants to complete a survey about their opinions on various topics, such as premarital sex and legalizing marijuana. Participants were then asked to estimate what percentage of their peers would share their opinions. The researchers were interested in whether the participants would overestimate the percentage of people who shared their opinions, and to what extent.

In Ross' False Consensus Effect study, the results showed that participants tended to overestimate the extent to which their attitudes and beliefs were shared by others. Specifically, participants were more likely to assume that others would share their opinions on more controversial topics, such as premarital sex or capital punishment, than less controversial topics, such as tooth-brushing habits. Furthermore, participants who held more extreme attitudes tended to exhibit an even greater false consensus effect. Overall, the study demonstrated that people have a tendency to overestimate the prevalence of their own beliefs and attitudes among others.

The study also highlights the importance of recognizing the potential for bias in our own thinking and perceptions of others, and the need to actively seek out and consider diverse perspectives. Overall, the study suggests that people may have a natural inclination to assume that others are more similar to themselves than they actually are, which can have implications for communication, decision-making, and social interactions.

Ross' False Consensus Effect study had several strengths. Firstly, it provided valuable insights into the cognitive bias of false consensus. Secondly, it employed a robust experimental design, including control groups and counterbalancing to mitigate potential confounding factors. Thirdly, the study used a diverse sample of participants, making the findings more generalizable to the wider population.

However, the study also had some weaknesses. Firstly, the sample size was relatively small, limiting the statistical power and the ability to detect small effects. Secondly, the study relied on self-report measures, which can be subject to response biases and inaccurate reporting. Lastly, the study had a somewhat artificial setting, which could limit the external validity of the findings.

Chapter 13 – The case of Henry Molaison

In 1953, Henry Molaison, known as H.M., underwent a groundbreaking surgical procedure aimed at alleviating severe epilepsy. At the time, the prevailing belief was that the hippocampus played a central role in the generation of epileptic seizures. To test this hypothesis, surgeons, led by Dr. William Beecher Scoville, decided to remove parts of H.M.'s temporal lobes, including the hippocampus, in an attempt to mitigate his epileptic symptoms.

The removal of H.M.'s hippocampus had a profound impact on his life, primarily manifesting as anterograde amnesia. While his short-term memory remained intact, he could no longer form new long-term memories. This impairment significantly influenced his daily life, making it challenging for him to remember people he had just met, learn new information, or navigate through unfamiliar environments. Despite these challenges, H.M. retained his intellectual abilities, showcasing the specificity of the surgical impact on memory processes.

H.M.'s case had a monumental impact on the fields of psychology and neuroscience. The study of his condition provided unprecedented insights into the localisation of memory functions in the brain. By demonstrating the selective nature of the surgery's impact on memory, particularly the role of the hippocampus in forming new long-term memories, researchers gained a deeper understanding of memory processes. H.M.'s case became a cornerstone in the development of the dual-store model of memory, distinguishing between short-term and long-term memory systems.

However, the ethical implications of the study warrant consideration. H.M. was not fully informed about the potential consequences of the surgery, and the profound impact it would have on his memory and daily life. This case continues to influence discussions on the responsible conduct of research involving human subjects.

Printed in Great Britain
by Amazon